Questions for my Heart

journal belongs to...

© 2016 Ranch House Press
All rights reserved. Printed in the United States of America.

www.annettebridges.com

ISBN: 978-0-9981576-6-5

Journal Prompts

Questions for my Heart

1. If you could write a letter to your 15-year old self, what would you say?
2. What do you want to be remembered for?
3. Think about the last time you felt totally on top of the world. Where were you? Who were you with? What were you doing? What parts of that experience can you recreate today and every day to boost your happiness?
4. If you could choose one word to represent yourself now, what would that be? Too hard? Pick 3 words.
5. What things in your life should be non-negotiable but isn't yet?
6. What do you want to say YES to?
7. What 'I should do this' things are getting in the way right now?
8. Which season do you most look forward to? What does that season give you?
9. What 5 childhood activities would you love to bring back into your life?
10. Write all the things you associate with the word 'joyful'.
11. What 3 big adventures would you like to have this month?
12. What things are so fun to you that you never get tired of doing?
13. If you could have an infinite supply of just one thing, what would it be? Why that thing?
14. List 3 things you could ask others to do instead of doing them yourself?
15. What one thing could you add to your evening routine that would make a difference to your wellbeing?
16. What decision do you need to make today to feel more peaceful?
17. What feels out of balance in your life right now? How can you make things more equal?
18. I'm ready to forgive myself for…' Take lots of time in writing each one down.
19. List all the things you want to say NO! to.
20. What are you ready to stop feeling guilty about?
21. List 3 things you can do this evening to nourish your soul.
22. List the things you'd give up to be happy.
23. Make a list of 100 things you love to do, big and small.
24. What would your very own sanctuary look like? What would you have in it?
25. What is sacred to you?
26. If you had a box labeled 'DESIRE', what would you put in it?
27. What do you NEED to be doing with your life?
28. What one thing could you add to your morning routine that would make a difference to your wellbeing?
29. List 20 things that represent passion to you.
30. Describe 5 things about you that nobody knows.
31. What are you procrastinating on at the moment? What fears are you giving into?

color your world

ABOUT the CREATOR

Annette Bridges is an author, publisher and women's retreat host on a mission to help every woman realize her story is extraordinary, valuable and noteworthy.

She has published the *Color Your World Journal Series* and formed a journal club to provide community, support and tools for women to record their ideas, feelings, experiences, memories and all the important details of their lives.

Before writing books and publishing journals and coloring books, this former public school and homeschool educator spent a decade writing hundreds of helpful, instructive, and light-hearted columns published by Texas newspapers, parenting magazines, websites and bloggers.

Annette lives on a Texas cattle ranch with her husband John, dachshund Lady and lots of cows. She can drive a tractor but only if wearing a fresh coat of lipstick and it's not her pedicure day!

You can learn more about Annette's books and products, blogs and videos as well as her women's retreats and other events at www.annettebridges.com.

Look for her on social media, too!

MESSAGE from the PUBLISHER

The *Color Your World Journal Series* is a pathway to self-discovery. It's where you write notes to yourself. Be your own cheerleader. Give yourself encouragement. Tell yourself what you're grateful for. Celebrate you!

There are countless reasons to keep a journal including collecting favorite recipes, listing goals and celebrating every experience and every one that's near and dear to you. A journal provides a home for the memories and lessons learned that you never want to forget.

Why a niche journal?

If you're anything like me, you have a journal (or even two or three journals) where you write anything and everything about anything and everything. My challenge comes when trying to find something I've written. I flip and flip through the pages of my two, three or four journals trying to find whatever it is. I never remember which journal I wrote down my whatever's!!

The solution? A niche journal! A journal that has a specific focus and theme! A journal where you can record your ideas, inspirations and things you want to remember in the appropriate journal.

Why big unlined paper?

Because big unlined paper is needed to record big ideas, dreams and memories! You need room to grow, stretch and expand. You need space to think beyond the confines of what you've always done, to pursue new dreams, discover your power and reimagine your purpose again and again. You need pages without lines and limitations to reconnect with your creative, perfectly imperfect self.

Plus, big unlined paper gives you space for more than words. You have plenty of room to doodle, draw or post photographs and clippings, too.

Why color is important?

When you journal, use colored pens and markers! Your world doesn't happen in black and white. Your life should be lived and written about in many colors. Even dark and sad memories feel lighter and brighter when told in color.

Journaling in color affects your mood and perception of your world. Colors evoke calm, cheer and comfort. Using color can lift your spirit and inspire your imagination. You may be surprised by all the beautiful benefits from adding more color into your life story.

When journaling, give yourself time to listen to your heart and reflect. Breathe in the moments. Feel. Be quiet. Let yourself be totally and thoroughly present with your thoughts. Let your heart transform you and teach you new insights. Open your mind to consider new ideas and possibilities. You may find that what your heart teaches will be life changing.